S. I. Darling

Messages from the watch tower

S. I. Darling

Messages from the watch tower

ISBN/EAN: 9783337810870

Printed in Europe, USA, Canada, Australia, Japan

Cover: Foto ©ninafisch / pixelio.de

More available books at **www.hansebooks.com**

PREFACE.

O—" Reapers of Men," let us reason together!
  Fling down the sharp blade that brings sorrow and waste,
Then pause till the clear, chiding voice of the spirit
  Hath questioned and judged of this murderous haste

The harvest is small, for the hands have been many
  That grasped at the sickle ere scarce had been sown
The seed that should slowly have grown to its fruitage
  And swelled with its richness, each plant with its own

Have pity, O Reapers! the Lord of the harvest,
  The Spirit that fills all duration and space—
The life of all things—called you not with your sickles
  To slay in unripeness each suffering race

The Spirit is speaking through lips that are mortal,
  And calls to account the thought o our hearts;
Mankind reaches upward and throngs of swift angels
  Float through where the curtain grows thinner and parts.

The words that I give unto me have been given;
  My voice been attuned to the needs of the world,
Where poverty, sorrow and folly and weakness
  Are jostling each other till brothers are hurled

Far down the black depths to red crimes and repentance.
  So blame not the measure that moans like a dirge;
But lighten the sorrow, remove the temptation,
  That man may be born without passions that surge,

Like over-full rivers, toward woe and destruction—
  Be lovingly welcomed, so, born without hate,
Forever beyond all the need of atonement,
  To murmur no longer and question his fate.

LUPA.

MESSAGES

—FROM THE—

WATCH TOWER.

To Parker Pillsbury.

A "Voice in the wilderness" evermore chants,
  "Prepare ye, prepare ye the way of the Lord !"
And ever the Few give heed and obey,
  For few are the sentinels waiting for day;
The Many still dream of the coming of light,
  And mock at the shepherds that watch by the night—
The few who have welcomed the star of the morn,
  And sought the low couch where their Savior was born,
Who speak to dull ears, and forsaken, unknown,
  Await the sharp hour of their torture alone—
Yet ever the Voices, unheard by the crowd,
  Are crying, "Prepare ye the way of the Lord !"

Would love wrap the body in trappings of state,
  And tempters dare whisper of kingdoms that wait,
With sorrowful gestures they wave them aside :
  "No, not of this world in its perishing pride
Is the kingdom I seek, yet the work that I do—
  The baptism I bring—all the earth shall renew;
And they who would reach toward the highest and best
  Must struggle in spirit, with grief for their guest;
For only to these cries the Voice of the Word :
  'Prepare ye, prepare ye the way of the Lord !' "

Dear friend, with a tender and reverent hand,
  We softly would touch the dear markings of care,
Would smooth on thy temples the silvery hair,
  And gladly, triumphantly, crown its soft waves
With glistening laurel, but almost we hear
  The loving reproach that was uttered before
By Jesus of Nazareth spoken once more.
  "Why call ye me good ?   There is none good—not one."
"Pause not by the way ; there is work yet undone;
  We sowed the good seed, now the reapers are near;
Waste naught of the harvest whose cost was so dear.
  Up, up, and to work, for the morning and noon
Already are here, and night cometh so soon ! "

O, Voice in the Wilderness, float to the heights
And gather the tones of the truths that endure;
  Then pierce to the depths of earth's falsehood and sin,
Where cunning and hatred, with clamorous din,
  Still wrangle like beasts that are hungry for prey;
O'ercome their harsh discord by whispers of peace,
  By faith in the future 'tis theirs to attain
When Eden, the Eden of wisdom, they gain.
  So long as the weak shall be held by the strong,
So long as the right shall be turned into wrong,
  So long may the ages re-echo the words :
"Prepare ye, prepare ye the way of the Lord ! "

O, faithful, tried Prophet, already the light
  That gleams from the higher life brightens thy sight;
The glow of that radiance blesses the east,
  And gladdens the uttermost parts of the west;
The cloudlets of dawn are *now* rosy with hope,
  And murder is hiding the knife and the rope;
The nations are seeking the way to be saved,
  The way, the salvation, the Few clearly saw,
From self and from forms, from unpurified law.

O, strong, fearless Spirit, a little time wait,
 And enter not yet at the heavenly gate !
The watchmen, the shepherds, gaze up to the sky—
 Still listen and wait, for the angels draw nigh,
And soon will be heard the glad tidings they bring,
 The song of " Good will " and of "Peace" that they sing.
Still wait till thine eyes have beheld the young child,
 And into thy face at baptism it has smiled,
And then, as earth fades from thy lingering gaze,
 Grown dim through its own grief's gathering haze,
May strength in thy tremulous hand yet remain
 To spread thy worn mantle o'er those that still kneel,
And watch by the tombs where their Saviors have lain.

The Watchman.

"What I say unto you, I say unto all, watch."

Over the sea in castled Spain,
Where the dark-skinned Moors fought hard and long,
From the arena's dust and din,
Dulling the martyr's dying song,
    Listening, we hear,
    Ringing and clear,
The cry of the pacing watch outside :
    "Alerto ! Sereno!"

On the alert for foes without,
For the slow approach or quick surprise;
On the alert for foes within,
Treason and dearth and coward cries,
    Watching alone,
    The turret's stone
Still echoes no word of his but these:
    "Alerto! Sereno !"

When, in our haste, we leave the tower,
And the warning cry stirs not our souls,
When we forget the pacing guard
Till o'er the walls the tide wave rolls,
    Till foes are within,
    Whose is the sin?
For still sounds the faithful voice outside:
    "Alerto ! Sereno !"

Only by those who watch is earned
The "Sereno" time, the after peace—
Need of that watch shall end when might
Triumphs no more and war shall cease.
    Then shall the skies
    Echo glad cries—
The shout of the watchman of the tower—
    "Triunfo ! Sereno !"

A Prayer.

O, Spirit of Justice! tell us where
Thy court is held and where the way
That leads within thy holy place!
Thy messengers have stirred the pool,
The tear-filled pool of human woe,
Till clutching hands, despairing eyes,
Pale, gasping lips and sunken cheeks
Arise from out its depths and plead
For hearts that have no voice to beg,
For help to save them from themselves.

We gaze in horror on the path
These wrecks have traveled, and we see
From mansion and from hovel, shapes
Of misery and vice and crime
Pour forth in long, unpausing lines:
They steal through secret alleys, led
By fierce desires that rage within,
And, eagerly or slowly, glide
To meet the future's sure remorse,
To meet the *angel* bending low,
In pitying watch, above the pool
And begging every sinking soul
To reach and grasp the offered help.

And yet, though cleansed and whole they stand,
What gain has come from fall and rise?
What wisdom planned the *need of wrong*?
If soul perfection comes to those,
And only those, who learn by sin,
Did He to whom the nations pray—
Jehovah, Allah, Jove or God,
The all-pervading Mighty One—

Gain thus the power to rule supreme ?
Why seek we then to smother vice ?
Why punish, as for deadly crime,
Those gaining thus eternal life?
If only spirits that repent
Are welcome in the heavenly home,
(As need of pardon most pertains
To him who carries deepest guilt)
The one gains most who sins the most.

We see men ask, cn bended knees,
Their God to lead them not within
The dazzling snare temptation spreads,
Then dig a pit for other souls.
They license wrong and then forget
That those who give and who receive,
And they who use the silver, all
Are partners in this game of death.
They keep the fountain springs of life
Impure, unguarded, rank and thick
With vile, inherited disease
Of body and of spirit ; then,
When causes have produced results,
They crush the fruit themselves brought forth.

O Justice! teach us to be just !
To seek preventive for redeeming grace:
Teach us to need no ransoming blood;
Show us that, Judas-like, we sell
The lives of others for a price;
That they who cause another's sin
Are guilty of that sin themselves;
That no atonement wipes it out,
But leaves a stain, a scar behind,
And that not only by our deeds,
But by our motives we are judged.

The End.

"At the last it biteth like a serpent, and stingeth like an adder."

Only an empty bottle,
Only an old brown jug;
Near them, a brimless hat-crown,
A pipe, and a broken mug.

Only a cheap pine coffin,
Borne to the Potter's Field—
Never a mourner followed,
Never an organ pealed.

Only the rain's low sobbing,
Only the wind's sad moan,
Told to the passing stranger ·
The drunkard had died alone.

Once there were friends around him;
Once he had hope and health;
Once was his manner fearless;
Once he had life's best wealth.

Now, have his trembling footsteps
Ceased in their shuffling round;
Now has his earth-life ended,
There, at that lonely mound.

"What brought about the beginning?"
"Who is to blame for the end?"
Only the tempting bottle,
Only the Judas friend

Now, is that Judas resting
Softly in cushioned ease
That, out of all life's riches,
Left to the drunkard these—

Only an empty bottle,
Only an old brown jug;
Near them a brimless hat-crown,
A pipe and a broken mug.

My Turn to Treat.

"My turn to treat," the dealer said,
"Come, bashfulness seems out of place,
On this, our nation's birthday, too,
In veterans who wore the blue;
Who met all dangers face to face;
Who never feared a shot or glass,
Nor turned aside to let them pass."

One fiery son of Erin moved,
Drew back as if he had not heard,
Then gazed far down the dusty street,
Where waving grainfields seemed to meet,
Clasp hands and sigh without a word.
"Come," jeered the crowd, "come, Larry, b'y,
The powther makes us shmokin' dhry."

At length he spoke, and through his words
A plaintive little quiver crept:
"It's hard to let the crather be
That locks out trouble, hides the key,
And tells him we have only shtept
Outside the door of Hiven's hall,
To tell St Pather whin to call."

He pulled his old worn coat aside,
And from its inner depths brought up
The picture of a merry girl
With coal-black eyes and glossy curls.
"'Twas Mary—*Say! what's in that cup?*
I'll take a dhrop, and yet I mind
'Twas this that made me eyes so blind.

"I thought no harrm to take a drink
Jist whin it plased me, or a frind
Brought out a jug to warrm the could:
I niver thought the girl grew ould
With frettin', or that she would spind
The evenings whin I wint away
Upon her knees to sob and pray.

"I didn't think she'd mind, but, b'ys,
One 'Fourth' she begged me shtay with her
She filt 'so lonesome like,' she said.
But I had whiskey in me head,
And was as snappish as a cur;
For Ned stood by so smilin' like,
I knew what he would say to Mike.

"(He once was swate on her, ye see,
But Mary threw the spalpeen by,)

And so I tould her hould her jaw;
I was the one to sphake the law.
But thin she shtarted in to cry.
No matter what I did, I say—
Min shlap their Marys ivery day.

."*Give me a dhrink, and curse yer sowl!*
Ye're like the Divil, now, me b'y.
The Divil wance was shnake, ye know;
Jist see the ugly spalpeen go
Out on your arm and hand! he's dhry,

"Give him a dhrop and toast his health!
Whin ould St. Pathrick drove thim out
He lift their ghosts behind to wink
And shtrike at us beyant the dhrink—
Begorra! but he's big and shtout!
'My Mary?' Whisht! I say she's dead,
She and the baby on one bed.

"I didn't kill her—'twas the dhrink—
Take it away!—no, hide it there—
Be quick! there comes me little girl,
With Mary's eyes and Mary's curls.
(Oh, blissid saints! will no one dare
To sind *her* where her mother wint?)
Whisht now! no mather what I meant.

'She walks as I did on the night,
Tin years ago, you called me in,
(The Divil take yer sowl for that,
Though 'twouldn't make him over fat
Afther 'twas physiced of its sin,)
And made me roarin' dhrunk for fun,
And then showed Mary what you'd done."

A silence fell upon the group
As Maggie's eyes sought each face there.
"Yis, darlint, yis, (hic) I'm sober, see?
Now, shtand up straight, and walk like me.
We (hic) 'll go up shtreet to take the air."
They staggered out—like him! too like,
The drunkard and his sin-marked child.

Sale of Indulgences.

OR

Liquor License.

Who'll buy? Who'll buy?
The price runs high—
The panting, sluggish, sickening breath,
Of that huge, sensual beast of death,
Which bloats and fattens on the stolen strength
It draws from shrinking veins until, at length
It festers, by its own hot vileness fired—
This leering demon, self inspired,
    Takes up the cry,
    "Who'll buy? Who'll buy?"
Its hydra heads are masked and hid
Behind the opened coffin lid
Where bloodless bodies lie within,
The victims of that sale of sin.

Who'll buy? Who'll buy?
The price runs high,
For wants are pressing, need is great;
Our chosen council for the state
Has pledged the gold that we, in turn, must pay,
Though hosts of shining angels bar the way.
We sell the devilish trade that thrives
On all the filth in human lives,
    Makes *Christians* cry,
    "Who'll buy? Who'll buy?"
Seeks Vice for Virtue, laughs at Shame,
Leaves naught of Freedom but its name,
Stabs blinded Justice, strangles Faith,
Steals even Hope's dim, mocking wraith,
And brings the first and second death.

Who'll draw the line?
Who longs to sign?
How dare we judge the mitred Pope,
Who sold for gold salvation's hope?
The soul was bidding then for life, not death,
While we would poison all a nation's breath,
And sanction this unholy trade,
Seal this unrighteous law that Greed has made.
Fling back the screen
That stands between
The open and the hidden ways!
Expose that game that Satan plays !
Strip off his masks, make dimness plain,
And with the blood-red mark of Cain
Brand him who buys,
And him who cries,
"Who'll buy! Who'll buy!"

The Sentence.

A glimpse into a court-room.   "Thou shalt not kill."

———

"Hanged by the neck until ye be dead—
Life is God's gift, so murderers must die—
'Eye for an eye' and 'tooth for a tooth'—
God grant the mercy we must deny."

They, from their safe, high place in the State,
Gather the proofs and follow each thread
Spun from the mass, then judge and condemn—
"Hanged shall ye be until ye be dead."

Gaze on the culprit shivering there !
"Heavy-necked son of passionate life?"
No, *that* is the *law* embodied in flesh ;
Here crouches murder beside this young wife.

See how her dark, wild eyes read each face!
Eyes that looked first on Italy's skies—
Mark how she clasps and wrenches her hands
When, in a pause, her babe feebly cries!

"Murdered its father?" Yes, so they say;
But, when the truth creeps forth to the light,
Justice may judge the deeds of the law—
May, when the strength returns to her sight,

Brand as the culprit him that lies dead.
Worse than the quick, sharp stroke that can kill,
Crueler far, is the torture that steals
Light from the eyes and life from the will.

Who will protect that suffering babe?—
Cursed by its father in every breath—
And when it calls for its mother, what tongue
Cares to respond, "we choked her to death?"

Glorious sign of progress 'twill be!
Wonderful things we build to revere!
There is a cross all mossy with age,
Scaffolds with dangling halters stand here.

Scarcely are fit for us, so men say,
Courts and the jails, the caucus and polls,
And in a term as juror or judge
Lurks a fierce harm to our sensitive souls.

Yet, when they choose, they try and condemn—
Try by the laws *they* make and approve;
Weigh by *their* scales and mark by *their* line,
Womanhood's weakness and guilt to remove.

What can she say why sentence of death
May not be passed as lawful and right?
God seems asleep, his messengers dead!
Call, and this echo comes back from the night:

"Hanged by the neck until ye be dead."
Shades of the past, arouse from your tomb!
Point with your spectral hand to the graves
Filled by man's violence, shrouded in gloom!

Tell him that Vengeance bringeth forth Fear;
That in its turn brings Vengeance again,
Crowding back Love and Faith from the world,
Torturing Hope by wearisome pain!

Tell him that "*as* we forgive," runs the prayer,
" May we receive forgiveness for sin;"
And, that the cup he measures in wrath
May be returned o'erflowing again!

Shame on the people that murder by law!
Shame on a law that strikes at a slave!
Shame on religion that sanctions the wrong;
Shame on an age that cares not to save!

Eyes that can see and ears that can hear,
Read the glad words on eternity's scroll,
Hear the grand chant of forgiveness and peace,
That through eternity's ages shall roll.

Her Defense.

"Neither do I condemn thee. Go and sin no more."

Sirs, I *am* what you call me, "a girl of the town."
Yes, a *girl*, though you sneer at my use of the word.
I'm degraded and vile, sure contagion and death;
Doubt, despair, and slow mockery lurk in the breath
Of the demon that holds me where never is heard
One faint whisper of home or of womanhood's crown—
The bright halo around the young mother's bowed head.

Though I am what you call me, "a girl of the town,"
Who or what forms the town, that indefinite thing?
Is it woman's own voice that demands the supply
Of the thousands on thousands of such ones as I?
And whose vileness pollutes me? what venom can sting
Like the poison man deals with a smile or a frown?
Did you know, you who play with the laws of the land,
That I marked the bright gold which you laid in my hand?

Do the eyes of your wife ever question your course?
And sometimes when the Press sports a virtuous tone,
And proclaims deadly war on the victims of sin,
Do you teach your young daughters how 'tis that we win
Sure protection for them at the price of our own?
As you're Christians, pray try the good rule Jesus gave,
Why not give your own girls some one's daughter to save?

Does a woman go wrong by herself? I would ask.
Are you sure it is wrong? We are needed, you say;
And I many times question what life is the best,
Since the faster we live it the sooner we rest.
We deny not our sin and we gather our pay,
But you'll find it a more than Herculean task
To make clean the foul sinks of society life,
Or to sanctify vileness by naming it wife.

I am proof of my words, for this unresting fire
Was a curse from my parents, bequeathed before birth;
Bring your daughters and wives, let them see, let them hear,
Let them think, and then judge.   Am I tried by my peers ?
Ye wise men of the law, self-styled lords of the earth,
There's a time surely coming, each moment draws nigher,
When our sins and their motives will come to the light.
Perhaps yours may grow dark to the clarified sight,
When the measure ye mete shall be given ye again.

And it might be that ours have been canceled by pain,
For the flesh still is weak though the spirit endures.
Ye may torture the body, the soul is not yours,
And despises your judgments, your solemn deceit—
Forms, pretentions but frail, like the God with clay feet.
Set the hounds on my track, you will watch where I hide ;
Whether sooner or later, will come to my side,
And it maybe, in time, and through sorrow, will learn
That together the price of redemption we earn,
That together we rise, or together we fall,
And the honor of each is the safety of all.

Sunday Legislation—or Not?

"The Sabbath was made for man, not man for the Sabbath."

No! strive no more to bring from ancient days
What feelings, motives or what laws were theirs,
They will not fit our ways, our minds, our times—
All these have changed, and like their change too well.

We decorate ourselves with cross and chain,
And, when a passing stranger labels them
The signs of pain and bondage, we but smile!
Yet, let the lighter hand of cunning spite
But lay its finger-tip upon our heads
And try to clasp the collar round our necks,
Or let the iron jaws of law but close
Unwontedly, the added weight, the press,
Becomes at once too grievous to be borne,
So much we love our own free life and will.

Draft laws, frame statutes—they're but forms;
The Spirit of the Age glides ever on,
And gives small heed to petty things likes these.
It leaves, upon its old, forsaken track,
Some line upon a stone, some solemn word,
Like ancient Mede and Persian law for strength,
And only laughs when trembling fingers point
To where, unheeded in the dust, it lies.
At times it toys in wanton, mocking mood,
With codes and tables, like a child at play,
Turns this for that, proclaims the last as first,
And daringly does wrong so harm may come,
To test the anger of the Unseen Powers.

So people are both worse and better than their laws—
Those yielding gloves that shrink to any hand,
Quite useless if the strong, the living flesh
Fills not its parts, and quickly thrown aside
If but their tissues bind or mar the work.

Yet lose not faith in final human good.
The world grows surely better day by day,
Through ever seeking for the hidden truth,
Through questioning in doubt and pain.
If all the nations be as one, some day,
In time and measure, speech and thought and hope,
In faith and in baptism, why should we
Mark all the rest by our one little line?
What matters it which few and fleeting hours
Are set apart for worship, or what name
We give to their or our one day of rest ?
Let each keep friendly with his conscience still,
And bind no yoke upon his neighbor's soul
When Nature sounds a protest, for if God
Speaks not through living things he would not mark
The thrilling essense of the universe
On tiny blocks of transient, crumbling stone.

A Fireside Dream.

Written in 1889, when arguments for and against the union of Church and
State (or Religious Legslation) were agitating many minds.

The week of toil had worn away,
  And o'er the ocean and the land
  The evening came with peaceful rest;
  I mused betore the open fire
  With dreamy brain and idle hand;
  The days, the years, o'erfull were pressed
  With anxious care, yet clearer, higher,
The flames shot forth and held me there

With golden heavens and lurid hells,
  ('Twas strange how close, how like they seemed
  By just a shade of color told,
  By violence or calm defined!)
  And these like joyous sunlight gleamed,
  Like harps and crowns and streets of gold;
  Those, dark with horrors, glowed behind,
With hissing jets and forked tongues.

Then battles raged, and lightnings flashed,
  And, when they ceased, a city rose
  In sheltered peace, behind the whole,
  With walls and bridges, and on high,
  Just where the folded flames unclose,
  And, singly seek their destined goal,
  Through darkness to the upper sky,
A wondrous structure reared itself,

With dome, and spire, and minaret,
  And stately wings of sober gray.
  It grew, and fell, and grew once more,
  With cumbrous walls of varying strength,
  And though the wide foundations lay
  At equal depth, still as before
  The rising sections fell at length,
Upheld, repelled each other's wreck,

(As if in anger that they came
  From common flame and common breath,)
  And showed the yawning, hollow heart,
  Where each with jealous pride drew back,
  And set again that trap of death;
  Yet knew not each had wrought its part,
  Was sharer in the common lack
Of clasping union in the heart.

  Then voices called for iron strands,
  To bind the towers round about—
  "For me and mine," each builder said,
  And as the girdle strained and bent,
  The added pressure from without
  Brought quicker ruin on his head;
  Yet still he knew not what was meant,
Read not the lesson of the past.

Then spoke the solemn voice of Time:
  "Ye bind the form—the soul has fled—
  The crumbling temple of the past
  Is now an empty tomb—too late
  Ye seek the living with the dead.
  Ye cannot bind the spirit fast,
  Nor save the Church by hoops of State;
This clasping with unyielding bonds

Is needless when the heart is sound,
  Is useless when 'tis full and strong;
  Nay, worse than useless, for they fall
  In melting fragments on the wrecks
  Creative fire has tried, where wrong
  Spreads, shade by shade, its funeral pall,
  And temples shrivel into specks,
For life is greater than its forms."

Then silence seemed to follow sound,
  And fill itself with mystic forms,
  With strange, wierd fancies; shadows grew,
  And fled in fearful, ghostly play,
  As when the gathering summer storms
  Send silent guards, as if to view
  Earth's treasures ere they're were swept away,
  Then draw them back and, in the hush,
The raging, swift destruction comes.

The hollow echoes of the vaults
  Gave back the ancient edicts then,
  Till dome and spire and minaret
  Returned the words and seemed to shout,
"Proclaim the banns of Church and State."

A surging concourse filled the space,
  And noted not the trembling towers;
  Each faction strove to lead the whole
  And shape that union's wedding rites.
  As struggle good and evil powers,
  So struggled these; as oceans roll,
  So rolled and leaped to greet the heights
  These warring discords, wave on wave,
  Till, shuddering, I seemed to rise
High o'er the battle's smoke and blaze

And listen from above, and there
  Few words of each I clearly heard:
  These formed a chain like finest gold,
  With each bright link a chiming bell,
  And all the breadth of air was stirred,
  As, peal on peal, the music rolled,
  A promise rounding each loud swell,
Of hope, of freedom, and of peace.

It surged across the billowy plain,
  It gathered up the ocean's moan,
  It echoed from the mountain's crest
  And touched with joy the thunder's knell;
  It blessed each soul that mourned alone
  And sang to weary ones of rest,
  A promise still in each loud swell
Of hope, of freedom and of peace.

Blind eyes were opened wide to see;
  The mute remained no longer dumb;
  For o'er and o'er the message rang—
  "*I hereby do forbid the banns!*
  Thus from themselves the fiat comes
  And mingles with the song they sang
  Who woke the shepherds of the plain
With "Peace on earth, good will to man!"
    *   *   *   *   *   *

The fire was smouldering on the hearth;
  The church was coal, its priests were smoke;
  And fitful darkness hid the whole ;
  Yet all the quivering air seemed filled
  With messages the conflict spoke—
  With strength and warmth that feed the soul—
· And all life's croaking cares were stilled.
So evening passed in peaceful rest.

"The Poor Ye Have Always With You."

WHY?

"When the wicked are multiplied, transgression increaseth."

———

Why nestles this sister in velvet,
While that one still shivers in rags?
Why idles this brother in riches
While that one through poverty lags?

If stripped of their rags and their velvet,
Where then would the difference lie?
In word, or in tone, or in gesture,
Or even the light of the eye?

Lo, these are but masks, are but garments,
The outward expression of soul;
The spirit that lives, thinks and suffers,
A part of the infinite whole

That works though 'tis hindered and baffled—
Works upward through ages of pain—
Weaves ever anew its torn garments,
And labors anew at each stain.

What withers the scarcely-made venture,
Or blights the long service at last,
While other risks sail to their harbor
And wait till the storm has gone past?

Do elements battle against us,
Or far-distant stars rule our course,
Or shall we yet seek for the causes
In some nearer fountain of source?

Still back of the form lies expression,
And back of expression the soul
That springs to its work as the lightning
Will answer its opposite pole.

O, wondering mothers and fathers!
Creation is mirrored in you;
Think, study and learn life's great problem
And then to your knowledge prove true!

Like wide open books are the children,
Where mothers may read, if they will,
The records of long-secret warfare,
Or trace the dear words " Peace, be still!"

And fathers may follow their weakness,
Their follies and crime to their fruits,
May nourish their virtues embodied
Or sigh over lives fit for brutes.

So long as the germ holds the essence
Of tyrannous scheming for gain,
So long as 'tis nourished by cravings
For wealth beyond power to obtain,

Or fed upon stolid endurance
With flashes of vengeful unrest,
So long will Dives feast to his sorrow
    And Lazarus linger our guest.

The Earth is The People's.

"The earth is the Lord's and the fullness thereof,"
We read in a scripture held sacred as old—
He speaks through his creatures and lives in their life,
So earth is the people's to have and to hold.

The whole, not a fraction, the whole, not a part—
For who hath created the ocean or land?
Who fashioned a mountain, or hollowed a vale,
Or moulded the granite by turning his hand?"

Who holds a clear deed that the powers of the air
Respect in the course of their out-rushing breath?
Whose mortgage holds good when the forces beneath
Arouse in the rage of destruction and death?

When, ages on ages, earth silently rolled,
When, atom by atom, it drew to its place,
What title to land was embedded in stone?
Whose name was tattooed on its stern rugged face?

All breath is but vapor, all flesh as the grass;
It droops and is gone, and the soul can retain
But essense, but spirit, the meaning and life
Of all that its servant, the body, may gain.

Then wherefore this battle for houses and lands?
Why eagerly grasp what another may need,
Demanding his strength or his life for your gain,
Demanding a harvest yet grudging the seed?

Ye heirs to the kingdom of freedom, of peace,
Oh, sell not your birthright for pottage, for dross?
The wages of greed will be worthless and vain
When cast in the balance of profit and loss.

How long will the children of Isaac contend—
The crafty, the favored, the Jacobs of earth—
With sad, angry Esaus too weary to prize
The glorious heritage his by his birth?

How often will innocence yield unto craft?
How often the husbandman, Abel, be slain
By slaughtering brothers all fevered with rage,
By cursed, and despairing, and wandering Cain?

"The shroud hath no pockets" has often been said,
Yet man in his eagerness, calls from the grave,
"'Tis mine and my children's forever and aye,"
Then sinks out of sight in eternity's wave.

O Cain! still thy brother's blood calls from the ground;
His keeper thou wast, with his weakness thy guilt.
The earth is the people's, yet cities of gold,
To cover the marks of thy crime, thou hast built.

"In Union there is Strength."

All the upper air is thrilling
  With a prophecy of change.
All the lower air responding
  Throbs with something new and strange.
Read ye not the wall's handwriting?
  Hear ye not the breakers' roar?
Feel ye not the spirit's warning
  Of a danger just before?

Seek the soul's most secret chamber;
  Cleanse each treasured relic there,
For the herald of the future
  Mounts the darkened, winding stair,
Loudly calls for proof of service
  In the line of human needs,
Brings the scale to measure motives,
  Balance promises and deeds,

And, with shining keys of knowledge
  Bound to twining cords of faith,
Brings creative fire from Heaven,
  Lights the pathway over death,
Shows electric bands enfolding
  All as one, both near and far,
Shows the brotherhood existing
  'Twixt the satellite and star.

Then shall man forget that union
  Bringeth life—disunion, death?
Would he fill his clay creations
  With the spirit's quickning breath,
Then must he, by combination,
  Learn the way to peace at length;
For the lesson of the ages
  Is, " In union there is strength."

Many Stories in One.

"Escaped ! Escaped !" the cry went forth,
    Then women shuddered and grew pale,
While children glanced, awe struck and still,
    Back toward what looked so like a jail.

Men left their work and talked in groups,
    Self-made police paced out their beat;
The *town* rose up to scent the track
    Of one crazed woman's wandering feet.

The days passed on, and word was brought
    Of something floating in the bay,
An unknown body at the morgue
    And, what is strange, the papers say,

They found upon her, roll on roll
    Of paper, brown and soiled and torn,
All written o'er They read the lines,
    Then laid the bit of pencil, worn

With picturing that life of woe,
    Within the lifeless hand, but saved
The story it had told so well,
    They wondered not at what she braved.

Read, you who live in light and warmth,
    In happy love and hopeful dreams,
And learn that not to *all* is life
    The unmixed blessing that it seems.

*   *   *   *   *   *   *

" No more sorrows, aches nor pains ! "
    I read and closed my eyes in thought.
. A vision grew from out the past
    And meaning from the present, caught.

Between the cities by the bay
  Well-locked within the Golden Gate
Which marks, with fort and echoing gun,
  The sunken bar, the hidden fate,

The ferry steamers met and passed;
  The rustling throng, in groups and crowds
Or lonely watches, filled the decks,
  While overhead light, drifting clouds

But made more blue the summer sky;
  Life seemed an oft-repeated strain
Of melody, till, in a pause,
  A discord brought a thrill of pain.

The tone grew loud, then died away
  In shivering echoes, that the few,
Of all those hundreds, kept or heard—
  (For grief is old but joy is new.)

Half hidden from the light of day,
  For fear of saddening youth and health,
Down where the din might dull the sounds,
  For fear of vexing silken wealth.

A mounted cage with guarded door
  Held, not wild beasts, but fellow men;
And ever as the discord swelled,
  A woman's eyes glared from this den.

A woman's fingers grasped the bars,
  A woman's voice flung out the words
That after-years brought from the waves
  Wild as the cry of wild sea birds.

"O, no more sorrows, aches nor pain!"
  Again and yet again it came,
As now, upon the crumpled page,
  Line after line read still the same.

Poor, weary soul! perchance she caught
   A glimpse of rainbow in the rain,
A prophecy, but now fulfilled,
   Of life without the grief and pain.

Come read the lines with me and feel
   The long, slow agony of years,
The dying hopes, the self reproach,
   The dull, hard grief too dry for tears.

*   *   *   *   *   *   *

"You wish that my love was outspoken
   As it was in the days that are past,
And ask why the old time devotion
   To the end of my life could not last.

"And yet, if I tell, you'll be angry,
   Just as if I had meant to offend.
If only you'd question me kindly,
   And would patiently hear to the end,

"I'd remind you of how in my girlhood
   I was dreamy and quiet and shy;
'So innocent', ever you called me--
   I could be your 'good angel;' and I,

"So useless aforetime I fancied,
   Was rejoiced to be shown my life work,
And gladly I knelt for my burden,
   Throwing back all the fears that will lurk

"Within the weak heart of the timid;
   For my faith in your love was so strong
I thought that with me for your helper,
   You would nevermorᴜ ꞵre to go wrong.

"I thought you could see that the right way
  Was the one that looked right unto me:
Though narrow the pathway we traveled
  That we closer together should be.

"Before you reproach for my coldness,
  To the innermost depths of your soul
Look down—Is it swept there and garnished?
  From the tomb of our youth let us roll

"The stone, while we tearfully enter,
    In a search for the Lord who has died.
'Not here with the dead—he has risen.'
    Let us look at his shroud side by side.

"Of thoughts, words and acts it is woven;
  Every hour, as it silently sped,
As silently broadened this garment
  Till it furnished a robe for the dead.

"See you any promises broken?
  And which side has the most, yours or mine?
Read you that it might have been better
  Had you heeded those prayers of mine?

"When, long years ago, I besought you
  To abstain from the maddening drink,
"Respect before love" said my nature,
  And you'll drive it away if you drink."

"And our boys—shall I teach them their father
  Has a right to do that which for them
Is wrong? Shall the cheeks of your daughter
  For your fault e'er be reddened with shame?

"Read on; does it say my petitions
    Were so lovingly granted, my years
Have passed like a hymn of thanksgiving
    And my eyes been unclouded by tears?

"A horrible dread ever present,
    Hints of darkness, despair and of death,
The ruin of home and of children—
    All the woes held in alcohol's breath.

"That hideous black thing in the cupboard,
    Running over with slow writhing snakes
That were nourished on curses and groanings
    And tears wrung from bitter heart-breaks,

"Is surely a thing of my fancy,
    For you would not so torture my heart.
You promised to love and to cherish
    Forever, till death did us part.

"The scales may have dropped from your eyelids,
    So read on and I'll leave you alone.
Perhaps our two lives may grow brighter
    When the Lord shall come back for his own."

Again read on, then clasp the babe
    Whose perfect form and loving ways
Are one unending joy, and think
    Of that poor mother's hopeless days.

*   *   *   *   *   *   *

"The mark of Cain was on the child,
    Set there before his form had birth,
The mark that sent him from his kind
    A hated wanderer o'er the earth.

Not from his parents did he take
His massive neck and heavy jaws,
The drooping lip and bloodshot eyes.
Men glibly talk of nature's laws

As if they knew them all, and yet
The fruit will mildew on the vine,
And unexpected sweetness spring
Where thorny brambles loop and twine.

"Long since a murder shocked the world
So unprovoked it seemed no voice
Could speak excuse or urge delay,
And so the law had left no choice.

"I, who had been that murderer's wife,—
(I married when scarce more than child,
And thought to hold this headstrong youth
Who only chafed and grew more wild.)

"I, who had been that murderer's wife,
The secret of my youth held fast,
Lest it should curse the Eden I'd found,
With serpent-hissing from the past.

'Yet still the specter would not down,
Each tongue described, each pen portrayed
The features, words and ways of him
Who dragged me through life's deepest shade.

"So, when my child was born, his child
Whose love had brought my happiest days—
It grew that other's image, then
The air seemed filled with thickning haze.

"And somewhere in that clinging mist,
My love, my joy, my hope, was lost.
My life's web knotted—and in vain
I try to get the threads uncrossed."

*   *   *   *   *   *   *

"Comfort was poised on its many hued wings,
Awaiting my choice for its stay or its flight;
Duty crept close and demanded my care,
Allowing no respite by day or by night.

"Choose! Could I choose while stern Conscience stood by
And gazed at the past when the seed had been sown
That, unnoticed, a horrible harvest had brought
Which now I must gather in sorrow alone?

"*Can* you love Duty, you steady and strong,
Who march where it leads you and shrink from no pain?
O I *did try*, but I longed to go back
And rest in the shadow of Comfort again.

"Life seemed so strange, so unequal and hard!
'Twas all a mistake; 'twas no sin; why should I
Suffer so much when another could laugh
And banter with Duty while Comfort stood by?"

*   *   *   *   *   *   *   *

"So you think I am sad without reason;
    That I foolishly moan and cry;
That I willfully shadow the sunshine;
    That for pastime I sob and sigh?
And you sometimes will carelessly wonder
    Why so often I pray to die.

If you'll cease your gay laughter a moment,
  And will listen, I'll tell you why:
'Tis because, on the veil of the future,
  Like a painting that hides the sky,
I see shadows of coming sorrow,
  Of a woe that is drawing nigh.

"Careless eyes see it not, and the vision
  Flashes back to its spectral place,
Where all things are as dreams scarce remembered,
  Or like ghosts of a haunting face;
Yet I feel, as each sad moment lingers,
  As the hours cling to life, and pace
In a line, like dead Joy's sad mourners,
  That Trouble will win the race;
That no power can destroy the wierd picture,
  Or the depths of its shades erase;
That its coming fulfillment is certain
  As the darkness, or time, or space.
So reproach me not now for my sadness,
  Nor the course of my blessings trace,

"For the weight of the world seems upon me—
  All its woes, all its follies and sins—
And I see that the strong rule the weaker,
  See that might is called right, and wins
By the method most cunningly watchful,
  That devours e'er a brother begins;
That will live on the breath of another;
  That will murder and call it law.
' *Tis the creed of the tyrant*, that surely
  Will be tried by the Heavenly law;
Then what heart will be void of offences?
  And whose hands will be be clear of stain,
When we stand face to face with our conscience
  And the secrets of life grow plain?"

          *   *   *   *   *   *   *

If only my daughter knew
How her mother's heart is aching
She would soon forget her own young grief,
For the woe the old heart's breaking;
For 'twas hers, my child, before 'twas yours !
Your sorrowful hours she, too, endures,
But she dare not look in your wistful eyes,
Though every glance is a precious prize;
And she dares not answer that pleading look,
For she reads it all like an open book;
And the sad reproach in your lingering gaze
But returns too keenly the olden days
When her life was young and she longed in vain
For a dream that never would come again
When she woke to find that the charm of the ring
Had summoned a horrible, brutish thing.
So your mute appeals for love's caress
Stab my heart again with the smothering pain.
The years of your life are the years of my woe,
And 'tis part of my penance to always know
I cursed the child I had hoped to bless.

" 'Tis a hard, hard thing when a mother pleads
For her own child's pardon for giving it life !
    And I love you so
    I must not show
That I care to have you near me;
    I had better frown
    Than drag you down
To the depths where you might fear me.
    And you must not care!
    O, if I dare
Fall asleep and never waken!
    If I only knew
    I'd soon be through

This dreary war of feeling!
    Will there come *no* change?
    Myself seems strange
With a horror past revealing.

Existence worries, wearies me, and life,
With all its causes and effects, seems only strife.
Why may I not resign it all and rest?
Why do they tell me that would not be best?
And yet, my child, your pleading eyes
Look up to mine with sad surprise,
And yet you moan, 'If only mother knew!'
O, who will give me strength to bear and do,
So that my precious daughter may not know
Whether the wheels of life run fast or slow?
    It would grieve her so—
    Don't let her know!"

     *   *   *   *   *   *

And last of all a little scrap
   All blurred and blotted as by tears—
A few sad words, and yet they told
   The dreary misery of years.

You say the blots were salt sea waves
   That murmured 'round her where, too late,
They found her floating with the tide
   Straight toward the Golden Gate.

Well, have it so—it matters not,
   But watch and pray and work to save
The helpless ones from lives like this,
   Or grudge them not the rest they crave.

     *   *   *   *   *

" It was terrible out in the darkness,
    Lying unpitied, alone,
With despair crouching somewhere unspeaking—
    The air filled with ghosts of a moan.

" At the dawning the shadows had gathered
    And crept to their place in my heart,
Yet again, at the coming of midnight,
    In ghostly procession to start

" And o'er lap their broad wings round my corner,
    Growing darker with each added day—
For Faith has forgotten to whisper,
    And Hope fled, affrighted away."

*   *   *   *   *   *   *

Escaped ! ah yes, escaped, we hope !
    It cannot be that "Over There"
She still must wrench at iron bars,
    Again gaze, wild eyed, at despair.

So close the eyes and fold the hands—
    The sights they shrank from all are past,
And tender spirit hands have clasped
    Those seeking ones in love at last.

In the Whirlpool.

I saw, within a stream, a whirling eddy caught
  Between two jagged rocks that almost met ;
It raged, and foamed, and turned upon itself, and beat
  Against the deep-set stones with ceaseless fret.

Exhausted by the plunge, it sullenly rolled on
  In heaving waves, yet backward threw a spray,
Of vengeance or forgiveness born, I knew not which,
  Above the boulder which had barred its way.

And ever as the current poured from fountain springs
  And started on its long, predestined course,
It sought the fearful pitfall it rebelled against,
  Impelled by inner and by outer force.

I wondered at the power, unseen but not unfelt,
  Which holds all weaker promptings in its grasp ;
Which draws unto itself all motion and all life
  And folds it in a still, resistless clasp,

Soon (changed, not lost, its grosser garment left behind,)
  To float, upborne by that, repelled by this,
Where finer essences and rare, etherial forms
  Reach forth, absorb, and mingling, bring the b

Of wondrous, resurrected life to earth again,
  Yet never, for a moment's breath, beyond
Where this unspeaking, uncrowned power must be obeyed ;
  Where elements could break or choose their bond,
  *   *   *   *   *   *   *   *
I saw, within the stream of conscious human life,
  A current that was destined from its source
To alway seek the whirlpool, beat eternal stone
  And hurry toward the leaps that bring remorse,

And sullen, heaving discontent, regretful pain,
   Which melted into tears and almost hid
The rage and depth and darkness of the crouching spring,
   And, momently, its fateful acts undid.

Yet still no backward glancing, moans, nor tears, nor prayers,
   Could turn that spirit from its destined course ;
It sought, then whirled about, the fatal rocks
   With dashing, feverish, or dark despairing force.

Again I wondered at the mighty unseen power
   Which held the current to its fateful track ;
Which kept the hardened rocks within its eager reach
   And left no choice between the fall and turning back.

Poor craving life, consuming self, yet unconsumed,
   Hold fast to hope ! The law that seems so cruel now
Is slowly drawing all the grosser elements
   That form the load beneath whose weight you bow,

And still will draw until at length the finer part,
   The soul, with its eternal powers, will rise
By this same law to kinship with angelic forms,
   Above the whirlpool and the cloudy skies,

Where all the complex plan of lite grows grandly clear,
   And in the calmness of creative peace
Dispersing blessings will return to bless again,
   All maddening leaps be past, all raging cease.

The Alkali Plains of Life.

There are lonely spots that are sometimes found,
    As humanity flows and ebbs,
That would seem to be only breaks and knots
    In the threads of creation's web,
        Or an after-thought, or a work undone,
        Or neglected task that is just begun,
So dry and caustic, silent and bare,
With not a song-note stirring the air,
As though accursed for the "primal pair."

Not a fragrant, tender and lovely thing
    Struggles forth from the grudging earth;
But the coarse, thorny plants, and wild, bitter sage
    In these desolate lands have birth:
        Yet the sage draws life from the stinging soil,
        And the bitter drops in their upward toil
Are changed to healing within its veins.
When bursting springs meet the pitying rains,
Some day the earth will have lost it sting,
Some day a golden harvest will bring,
Some day the desert with life shall ring.

*   *   *   *   *

There are lonely souls that are sometimes found,
    As humanity flows and ebbs,
That would seem to be worse than breaks and knots
    In the threads of creation's web;
        Worse than after thoughts of a work undone
        Or neglected task that is just begun,
So dry and caustic, silent and glum—
To all good things they seem to be numb,
To all that's musical deaf and dumb.

Yet the bitter life will to sweetness turn
  In a time that is drawing near,
When the long-pent sorrows have burst their bonds
  And are mingled with pitying tears
    From the eye that has opened to brighter light
    And has learned to read nature's essons aright,
That the bitter cures and the caustic heals,
And the dry, fierce heat the rare vase anneals.
Some time these souls will have lost their sting,
Some time a golden harvest will bring,
Some time these spirits with joy shall sing.

To Emilie Morsier.

[Who in behalf of the women of France proposed an International Peace Council
to be composed of women.]

Women of France, our Sister Republic,
Echo, on echo your call shall repeat
Nation to nation send ringing hosannas,
And angel with mortal clasp hands in their joy
Over the continents, over the oceans
Long have been hanging the storm clouds of war
Lightnings, thunders, tornadoes and darkness
Repeated in spirit to torture anew.

Long have the few been devouring the many,
Wasting their substance, their strength and their lives;
Claiming divinely appointed commissions,
They strike in the name of the Preacher of Peace.
Oft has the saber been pointed and sharpened,
Oft has the cannon paid tribute to death;
Always the mother-heart mourns its lost treasures,
Nursing a curse that returns in new births.

Now the Commander, the Spirit of Progress,
Calls for a halt in the fierce, onward rush;
Swords must be sheathed and the war drums forgotten,
Then man will grow gentle and woman can rest.
Reveilles sound, and the hosts are awaking!
Rank upon rank of brave mothers in line
Strengthen the arm that is rocking the cradle
With blood that is fresh from the warm heart of love—

Love that would shield the weak ones from oppression,
Love that refuses to bear with a wrong.
Man waits not forever when woman dares venture—
The knight fought for tokens, the brave for reward.

Woman, wherever you live, love and suffer,
Bless the brave heroes that stand by your side;
Heed the " Appeal " that comes over the waters,
Till war, want and famine are banished from earth !

Women of France, our Sister Republic,
Echo on echo your call shall repeat !
Nation to nation send ringing hosannas,
And angel with mortal clasp hands in their joy.

"Be Still,"

Calm the soul to list'ning silence,
  For the Spirit draweth nigh !
Hush all noisy, warring tumult
  Lest it sadly passeth by !

In the still, white heat of feeling
  Lies the power that moveth souls;
For they listen in the silence
  Where eternal spirit rolls

Through the measureless expanses,
  Holds each atom and each sun
In its ever onward current
  'Round the conscious life—the One—

Till they learn angelic anthems,
  Catch the echo of the tone
That can harmonize all discords,
  That is learned by each, alone—

Lone and silent, yet communing
  With the universal soul;
One, yet blending in that oneness
  With the universal whole.

The Electric Rule.

Though Saviors have lived and have suffered and died,
And prophet and priest have gone down side by side,
Their mournful eyes asking "Why seek ye my life
For teaching and living the gospel of peace,"
Still the struggle goes on, still the spirit of force
Forms statutes and breaks them the same as of old;
Still the voice of the world in its darkness and pain
Cries "Tear down the damp walls, let the light shine again!
We are cramped and deformed in our bodies and minds,
And our freedom is smothered in creeds and in laws."

The Self-Seeking Rule and the pure Golden Rule
Were foes, deadly foes from the first, so men say;
That selfhood must yield to that heavenly law
Ere earth can awake to the heavenly day.
So the righteous have toiled from the ages of yore,
They have urged, they have forced from their own precious store
Rarest treasures of faith, priceless visions of hope
On the brain and the soul that rebels at the gift.
"What is truth unto me should be truth unto you,"
They will cry in the haste of their unselfish zeal.

Should camel and lion divide their scant food,
What gain would there be to the general good?
The carcass would lie by the camel unused,
The hay would best serve for the young lion's bed.
The swift minnow might offer its home to the bird,
And the bird might entreat of the minnow to share
Its light swinging nest and its merriest song,
And its long, southward flight through the clear, upper air,
But the change would bring death to the generous twain;
What was meant for a good would end only in pain.

So still is the rule but the measure of self
On a higher line, and the wonder will come
If ever the consciousness loses itself—
If sometime it reaches existence so great
It loses the marks of this trial-filled state—
Can forget all the weakness, outgrow all the faults
That the hard, life-long struggle for bread now exalts—
Can so mingle itself with Omnipotent Cause
That the subject shall grow to be ruler of laws,

When life's first and last, the Electrical Rule,
That calls for no priest and is learned in no school,
The true law of *growth* of each soul toward its best,
Without forcing or check, shall be known and confessed;
When each life, like a flower relieved of a weight,
May outfill its own stature, though tiny or great,
And as happier ages glide into the past,
Every stature grow *nobly angelic* at last.

Backward and Forward.

Exultant, yet with panting breath,
Upon an eminence attained
We pause to rest,
To cleanse our garments from the dust
That had defiled the valley road
And, from the mountain's crest,
Gaze down the path by which we came.
Like silent tongues of hidden flame,
The sullen heat
Lights all below
In quivering glow;
With varying beat,
It pulses swiftly up the track,
As if it longed to drag us back.

On either hand, huge rocks are piled
That make the wilderness more wild,
And towering trees,
Grown old with time, yet unsubdued,
Scarce whisper in the solitude;
The tender, wandering breeze
Flits in and out, and lays a leaf to rest
Upon the mossy earth, and breathes, "'Tis best."
"And this is all,"
We think and sigh,
But from the sky
A fluttering call
Bids us take up our staff again,
For grander, higher heights remain.

        *   *   *   *   *   *

Almost we stand upon the ridge
Between the "This" and "That"—the bridge
That joins yet parts

The cycle gone and one to come:
The loud-voiced Past grows strangely dumb
    And lays its vengeful darts
In awe-struck, wondering silence, down
Beside the tottering cross and crown.

        The monarchy of force,
        The power of might
        To rule the right,
        Will soon have run its course,
And nations will forget the skill
Which armed and sent them forth to kill.

The hot pollution of the strife,
With all its waste of human life,
        Sinks, quivering, back;
From heights that hold the cooling shade,
From groves no feeble hand hath made,
        Across the downward track,
A message from high Heaven floats
In ringing, clear, unwavering notes:—
        "Arise, O Soul, and climb!
        For life is here

        And Heaven draws near
        Within the years of time!
Forget the sin that lies behind—
The greed of gain, which hates its kind—
Press on to that which lies before,
Where man shall learn of war no more! "

www.ingramcontent.com/pod-product-compliance
Lightning Source LLC
Chambersburg PA
CBHW031757090426
42739CB00008B/1051